The Boys in Black
by
Frank English

This work is registered with the UK Copyright Service.

Copyright © 2020 Frank English. All rights reserved.

2QT Limited (Publishing)

First Edition published 2020 by
2QT Limited (Publishing)
www.2qt.co.uk

Copyright © Frank English 2020

The right of Frank English to be identified as the author of this work has been asserted by him in accordance with the Copyright, Designs and Patents Act 1988

All rights reserved. This book is sold subject to the condition that no part of this book is to be reproduced, in any shape or form. Or by way of trade, stored in a retrieval system or transmitted in any form or by any means, electronic, mechanical, photocopying, recording, be lent, re-sold, hired out or otherwise circulated in any form of binding or cover other than that in which it is published and without a similar condition, including this condition being imposed on the subsequent purchaser, without prior permission of the copyright holder.

Typeset by Dale Rennard
Photographs used with kind permission

Printed in Great Britain by
Ingram Spark

A CIP catalogue record for this book is available from the British Library
ISBN 978-1-913071-85-1

Chapter 1

"Mummy?" Hugo asked as he scuffed his feet through the scrubland at the other side of their backyard fence in Crow Nest Lane. This was his first day venturing out with his mum on his favourite saunter towards Crowdon Woods since he had gone down with a particularly nasty bout of measles just after his sixth birthday party.

"Yes, my lovely boy?" his mother Gwen replied with an indulgent smile. "Now what is it you need to know?"

Almost without thinking, they stopped to pick dandelion clocks growing by the wayside as they neared the eaves of the wood.

"First, I've seen these flowers a lot out here," Hugo observed. "What are they and why are they white?"

"Put the white fluffy flower head in front of your mouth and blow," his mum explained.

"Why should—?" he began to question again.

"Just do what I suggest and see what happens," she insisted gently.

"Cor, look at that!" he gasped as the white flower head exploded, disappearing upwards and outwards. "Those little black spots look like they are floating down on para … shoots. What are they?"

"They are seeds that need to reach the ground." Then she added, "Why do seeds do that, do you think?"

"Do they do that to grow more flowers?" he puzzled, quizzing her face with a squashed little frown.

"Exactly," his mother replied.

"But, why para … shoots?" he asked again. "Is it because the wind blows them far and wide?"

"Excellent answer!" she said with a smile. "Clever boy. Now, I think we ought to go back home for a cup of tea."

"Do we have to, Mummy?" he asked, a disappointed tone edging his words. "I've only been out for a bit."

"That's just the point," she explained. "It's not long since you were very poorly. I don't want you to become tired like you were only a few days ago. All right? We'll come out again tomorrow."

"OK," he agreed as they turned to regain their back garden through their big fence gate. As he turned to latch the gate once his mother was inside, he felt a mild tingling start in the tips of his fingers, travel through his body and disappear almost as quickly as it had appeared.

He was about to tell his mum when he was distracted by a deafening cacophony of cawing crows at the edge of the woods. He turned sharply to see a black cloud lift out of the branches and head towards him in the garden. Not keen on this particular murder of crows, he dodged sharply in through the back door of the house.

"Did you see that?" his twin sister Betsy gasped. She was older than Hugo ... by one minute, and she always emphasised that whenever she wanted to appear clever. Girls, eh!

"That murder of crows?" he replied calmly. "They wouldn't have harmed either of us."

"A what of crows?" Betsy scoffed. "Murder? There is no such thing."

"Mummy!" Hugo called out.

"Yes, sweet boy?" she replied, popping her head round the kitchen door from the hallway. "What is it?"

CHAPTER ONE

"What's a group of crows called?" he asked, turning to face his sister. His eyebrows raised quizzically, knowing what his mother was about to say.

"But you know that already," Mum explained. "Why—?"

"I *know*, but Betsy doesn't believe I know," he interrupted.

"It's a murder of crows, of course," she said, before disappearing back into the hallway.

Betsy frowned and put out her tongue at her brother. "You didn't *know* they wouldn't hurt us. Did you?" she said, her hesitant voice showing her uncertainty.

"I knew instantly they passed over us," Hugo said with conviction. "I know also that the leader of the murder is called Seamus O'Croake, and he and his ancestors came from Cawk in Southern Ireland."

"There is no such place!" Betsy harrumphed indignantly. "You just made that up! How could you possibly know that?"

"I don't know how," he replied slowly, a deep frown growing. "As soon as they passed over, I seemed to just … know."

-o-

"That young yooman will have to be watched," Seamus O'Croake said to his eldest son, Corfc O'Croake.

"Why is that, then, Daddy?" the youngster asked, never sure whether his daddy was teasing him or being serious. "We don't know him – do we?"

"I do *now*," Daddy Seamus replied with conviction. "He is a very rare and special yooman. He is beginning to understand us, and we will need to keep a close eye or two on him."

"Why is that, Daddy Seamus?" Corfe asked, puzzled by his father's work.

"Can't you hazard at least a *wild* guess?" his daddy tried to explain patiently, but a great sigh slowly escaped his beak. "It was foretold many generations of crows ago that a young yooman would come among us and understand what we are as a nation. And I have a feeling deep in mi bones that this could well be THE ONE."

"What if he is THE ONE, Daddy Seamus?" Corfe puzzled. "What would that mean? And what difference would it make to us? It's not as if he would be ... living with us. Is it?"

Corfe hesitated, as if a grain of doubt was beginning to throw out shoots to encourage it to grow a little. It took only a very small shoot to set the process in motion and make him feel concerned.

"No, my ever-so-slightly disbelieving son, he won't be living with us *physically*," Seamus O'Croake explained. "But he will be living in our minds and hearts, and we will be able to learn from him."

"But, he's only a child-yooman!" his son protested. "How can he—?"

"It's called having ... FAITH!" Seamus cawed very loudly, making all his crow companions caw in unison as they recognised the word.

Corfe still didn't understand, even when his brother Carfe put his wing around his shoulder and tried to explain.

"As we don't know *all* the answers – *ever*, faith becomes a very important word," Carfe said. "If you don't *believe*, you will have a seriously troubled life, Old Chap. It's much the easiest course to follow. Only then will everything begin to fall into place."

"He's always been a questioner," Millie, Corfe and Carfe's mother said with a sigh as her son shuffled off, chuntering as he went. "He may understand – one day – but I'm not holding my breath. We need to be cawtious with that one."

Chapter 2

"Hugo! Quick! Come here!" Betsy shouted from the conservatory at the back of the house, which overlooked their large garden and the woods beyond.

"What is it?" Hugo asked as he appeared next to his sister, causing her to jump in surprise.

"The last tree in the woods, nearest to us?" she asked. "Is that a crow sitting on its own on that huge branch?"

"It is," Hugo answered calmly. "It's Seamus O'Croake's son, Corfe, and he's looking straight at us."

"How on earth can you know that?" Betsy gasped. "It's too far away to tell, surely, and how do you know? One crow looks very much like another as far as I can tell."

"Trust me," he replied. "I'm a twin. Watch."

He unsnecked the back door and sauntered across the path onto the lawn by the clothes pole near the back of the summerhouse. As soon as he stopped walking, the crow took off. Followed by several others, it headed for the ancient oak tree just the other side of the fence.

Betsy followed him out slowly and tentatively. When she reached him, she took up position close behind her brother to the accompaniment of a cawing cacophony from the gathered Boys in Black. Immediately Hugo raised his hand above his head, the noise from the throng stopped abruptly. One solitary bird lifted slowly from his knotty perch to land on the gate in the fence.

"Good morning, Mr Seamus O'Croake," Hugo started. "It's good to see you and your kin. I hope everyone is well."

"We certainly are, Young Master Hugo," Seamus replied in his gruff, croaking fashion. "I remarked yesterday that you had arrived at last. It is good to have our ancient lore finally come to pass. We have waited an age for this moment, so it behoves me to welcome you to our world."

"What's he saying?" Betsy whispered. "All I can hear is a raucous crowing noise."

Realising that he would have to act as a go-between, Hugo explained quickly what Seamus had said – to Betsy's disbelief and dismay. What did this all mean? A crow talking to a boy and the boy understanding everything it said? No chance! Or was there?

"Is your home world faring well?" Hugo asked his friendly corvid. "Cawk, I believe?"

"Indeed it is, young man," the stately crow replied. "Unfortunately, however, they have one or two knotty problems that need sorting out, and I believe it will take more than one of us to do it."

"Now what's he saying?" Betsy hissed, pulling her brother away a little from the group. "You have to tell me before I burst. It all sounds a bit … serious and important."

As Hugo explained, a shocked look stole into her face and her chin sagged almost to her chest.

"You cannot be serious!" she added, at last rediscovering her powers of speech. "Mummy won't let you – you realise that, of course. How *would* she allow you to travel to … Southern Ireland, is it?"

"She'll come *with* us, I can assure you," Hugo added calmly, with more self-confidence than she had ever seen in him before.

"And how are we to get to Ireland?" Betsy scoffed, still not sure whether he was serious.

CHAPTER TWO

"Do you think it might be helpful if I came to Cawk, Mr O'Croake?" Hugo asked the crow, ignoring what his sister had just asked.

"More than you could ever imagine," Seamus O'Croake assured him. "Tell your sister here that we understand her misgivings, and not to worry because we will protect you both."

"Protect us?" Betsy gasped once Hugo had explained Seamus O'Croake's words. "How on earth will *they* be able to protect *us*? We're humans and they're just … birds."

"It might be different for one bird, of course," Hugo replied, "but a thousand of them would be difficult to either ignore or prepare against. We will be fine. Mummy will be all right, too. Don't forget that Granny Essie and Grandpa Shylock live there, with Aunt Judith and Uncle Michael. We could stay with them."

"This is a mad scheme, Hugo, my crazy brother," Betsy sighed. "I have a feeling, however, that you seem to know what is expected of you by Mr Crow and his hench-crows, and that you are going to help sort matters out, no matter what."

"When do we need to be there, Mr O'Croake?" Hugo asked the chief crow. "Cawk City in County Cawk, did you say?"

"You'll come then, Master Hugo Mayes?" Seamus replied.

"Without doubt, Mr Seamus O'Croake," Hugo agreed without hesitation.

His mother had caught this conversation from her position behind the back door that her son had left ajar. A knowing smile began to play around her eyes and mouth corners, as she understood the importance of Hugo's position and growing relationship with this group of the cleverest of birds.

With a great caw, the Boys in Black lifted slowly into the air and wheeled away back to the woods by Badger's Hill to settle for the night in preparation for their journey to Cawk, Southern Ireland's largest county.

-o-

"Mummy?" Hugo said at tea, in that slow searching way he had of broaching a difficult question.

"Of course we can," she replied without hesitation.

"But I haven't—" he replied, puzzled.

"You don't need to," she interrupted. "I heard you talking to that large crow and, although I didn't understand *all* he said, it is clear there are problems that he and his people need sorting out. It is obvious that you need to see to what they ask of you. We will go and stay with your Granny and Gramps O'Keefe while you do what you have to do. We will be there with you to keep you safe."

"Mr O'Croake and his buddies will see to that, Mummy," Hugo explained carefully so as not to upset her. "Have we got any afters?"

"Only your favourite!" Mummy exclaimed theatrically as she magicked a large pie dish that had been covered out of sight on a side table close to her right elbow. "Now, you have three guesses before you are allowed any."

"Everything you make is my favourite, Mummy," he said, tapping his cheek with his little forefinger as she slid out into the kitchen. "But I'll have a slice of … sticky toffee pudding with custard, if that's all right."

"Tada!" Mummy chanted. She came back from the kitchen with a jug of steaming custard in her hand. "How did I know that was what you would choose?"

Both twins grinned and clapped their hands in glee, thoughts of that wonderful concoction rolling around their taste-buds.

What a wonderful way to finish an exciting day!

Chapter 3

Hugo and Betsy held tightly onto the railing around the ship's viewing deck, looking out over the Irish Sea, searching eagerly for land. At sea for only ten minutes out of Fishguard, they couldn't wait for the three-and-a-quarter-hour journey to Rosslare in County Wexford to be over. This wasn't because they didn't like the sea journey – they did – but because they couldn't wait to see Granny and Gramps O'Keefe, and Aunt Judith and Uncle Michael with their two children.

At just a year older than them, Mandy and Sean – also twins – were great fun to be with. As different as a bottle of vinegar and a glass of sparkling white wine, Mandy was the smart, funny prankster whereas Sean was serious and had his feet firmly on the ground.

"Are we nearly there, Mummy?" Betsy asked, hoping for a seriously positive answer.

"Well, if you consider three hours and five minutes nearly there, then yippee!" her mummy replied with a laugh. Betsy had always been impatient in everything she undertook. Her impatience was laced at times with overwhelming doses of scatterbrained-ness too, whereas serious Hugo couldn't be flustered, bored or impatient under any circumstances.

"Wow!" they heard a stranger say to another passenger in passing. "Never seen that before. Look! To starboard."

Everyone on deck turned to see a black cloud of crows keeping pace with the ship about a couple of hundred feet above the deck. Periodically, one single call let Hugo know that the Chief of Crows had brought his people along to watch over them.

"Seamus O'Croake?" Mother asked Hugo, who was standing motionless next to her, his eyes neither blinking nor looking away from his new clan.

"Indeed, Mother," Hugo replied slowly with a satisfied smile. "I *did* say they would look after us, didn't I?"

"Do you have any idea yet of the problems you will be facing when we reach Cawk?" Gwen asked her sometimes secretive son.

"Not been able to communicate with Mr O'Croake," he replied. "I don't think even *he* knows, other than there is some sort of a problem that we need to find a way to solve."

"Can we go down below and get something to eat now, Mummy?" Betsy asked her parents urgently. "I'm thirsty *and* hungry."

"Hark at you, with your 'down below'!" Mum replied with a giggle. "Posh or what!"

"Come on then, Poppet." Her dad Josiah led her to the stairs. "Café's down here. Pretty good food on offer, I hear. I'm a bit peckish myself."

"Is it all right if I stay up here for a bit?" Hugo asked as the rest of his family headed for the cafeteria.

Once they'd gone, he raised his hand and walked to the ship's stern, where nobody else was about. Within a few minutes, a crow drifted in to land on the guard rail. It was Seamus O'Croake.

"Good day, Mr Seamus O'Croake. Thank you for dropping in," Hugo greeted the crow he now felt he had known most of his life.

"Top of the morning to you, Master Mayes," the crow replied with a slight bowing of his head. "We have heard that the district council of County Cawk has issued a public notice that Glenbower Wood, where most of our kind live and nest, is to be cut down to pave the way and pay for housing for yoomans to be erected where the trees once grew."

CHAPTER THREE

"We can't let them do that, Mr O'Croake," Hugo insisted immediately. "That wood is ancient and is shrouded in history and legend. Perhaps we need to revisit its history and call back some of the legends to help in our quest to have the councillors rethink their decision."

"I like your thinking, young man," the old crow replied with a click of his beak. "However, you are the only person that can do that – and it must be on a full moon at the centre of the wood. Do you think you can bring that about?"

"It can be done," Hugo said confidently after a moment or two of thought. "It *will* be done, Mr Seamus O'Croake, Chief of all Crows."

The old crow looked deeply into the six year old's eyes and saw a deep mystical conviction he had never seen anywhere in his many years on this Earth. As he lifted off from the ship's railings to rejoin his crew, he knew this young boy's spirit was true. It originated in the lore and magic of long ago when honour, truth and respect for all creatures was king.

-o-

"Time for a cup of tea and a bite to eat, Poppet," Hugo's mum said. She stood by his side, her arm around his shoulders as she searched the faraway look in his face. "Penny?"

"Just thinking about tomorrow after what Crow O'Croake said a short while ago," he explained slowly.

"A short while—?" she asked, guessing that somehow he had communicated with the old bird.

"I walked to the back of the ship when no-one else was about and beckoned him," Hugo went on, matter of fact as ever.

"And?" his mother asked, not sure where this was leading other than to further concern and intrigue.

He paused for a moment and then explained to her what his friend had told him.

"Mmm," she replied, understanding now how much deeper the problem had become and worried that her son wouldn't be able to solve it. She was concerned, too, about how this impasse might affect *him*. "It will hopefully sort itself out in due course."

"Due course isn't an option, Mother," Hugo explained seriously. "I feel, however, that I might have a way forward."

"Which is?" she asked, not wanting to put pressure onto his little shoulders. He was a very smart and compassionate youngster but he was only just gone six, after all.

"I have this … feeling that we have to call on history to help us," he replied carefully.

"Surely history is what it says – in the past?" his mother said, a puzzled frown showing how much she didn't understand about how her son's mind worked. It seemed to her that he had learned to talk in riddles that *she* didn't understand at a very early age.

"I can't be more precise, Mummy, but we will see more clearly when we get to Glenbower Wood," Hugo explained seriously. "That's when we will know the size of the problem and the steps we need to take to sort it out."

"Anyway, time for something to eat and drink, my boy," his mother insisted. "Best part of an hour to go and we'll be landing in Rosslare."

"Rosslare, Mummy?" Betsy chipped in as she met her mother and brother in the cafeteria. "What's that?"

"The port where we will be docking," Hugo replied, as he eyed the food on offer at the counter. "It's in County Wexford. Then we'll be travelling south towards Cawk in County … Cawk."

CHAPTER THREE

"How do you know all this … stuff?" Betsy asked as she jiggled her feet while her brother took his time choosing what to eat and drink. "I don't know any of this, and I'm supposed to be your twin sister."

"I have no idea," he replied slowly. "It seems to just pop up in my head. Perhaps it's … magic!"

His mother caught his slightly ironic half-smile as he turned to find the table his dad was occupying near the enormous plate glass window. Hugo's hands were holding on tightly to his food-laden tray to counteract the pitching of the ship. He had no intention of relinquishing his food now that his stomach had started to rumble and grumble and growl.

His mum had long since given up trying to understand how his mind worked and how to follow his mature view on life in general. He usually solved problems in his head quietly twice before he opened his mouth once. And now … this!

"If Hugo's eating now, can I have some food as well, please?" Betsy butted in.

"Don't you think you've had enough?" Daddy Josiah sighed. "Two beef sandwiches, some chips and a cup of tea – oh, and two donuts?"

"They weren't very *big* donuts!" she complained as she eyed what her brother had on *his* plate. "Just a little … something? Please?"

Chapter 4

"Granny Essie and Grandpa Shylock!" Betsy shrieked with joy as she threw herself at her grandparents and buried her face in her grandpa's baggy cardigan. He flung his arms around her and drew her to his ample belly.

"Long time no see, my little pigeon," he cooed. "My, haven't you grown! Is this the granddaughter that was only knee-high to a baby crow the last time we saw her, Granny Essie? My word, how years fly and drag at the same time. Who on earth is that young man walking towards us with your ma and pa?"

"Hugo, Grandpa Shylock," the lad answered. "I'm Hugo, Betsy's twin brother." He never had got the hang of his grandfather's sense of humour – not his cup of tea, really.

"Stop teasing the lad, Shylock," Essie chided her husband mildly. "Haven't you grown, Hugo? As serious as ever, I see."

"Hello, Grandma," he greeted her, hugging her gently. "It's lovely to see you – both of you. Are we staying with you while we're here? And are Sean and Mandy likely to be here as well?"

"If you turn around now and look towards the dock house, you *might* see a couple of familiar faces," Grandpa Shylock explained.

"Mandy!" Betsy squealed as she flew to the dock house to throw her flailing arms around her equally excited ebullient first cousin. Her brother Sean walked over to Hugo and offered his hand in a restrained and quiet greeting.

"Grand to meet you, old chap," Sean said, nodding sagely as his face accommodated a gentle, genuine smile.

"Likewise, old friend," Hugo replied, glad to see his cousin again and relieved to be in his gentle but stimulating company. "You and I have something of concern to discuss this evening."

"Crows? Glenbower Wood, perhaps?" Sean guessed with a slight shrug.

"Nail on head, as usual, old man," Hugo said. "Seamus—"

"O'Croake?" Sean replied, equally assuredly. "Although I know about the Boys in Black, it is you who will have to seek the solution. I am simply here to help in your quest."

"And I believe I have that solution now," Hugo explained. "But we must discuss it later; if not tonight, then tomorrow."

-o-

The journey from Rosslare to Killeagh, to the north-east of Cawk, in Grandpa's old people carrier took the best part of two-and-a half hours, because of his 'steady' style of driving. Granny Essie called it 'slow'.

Their house was large by any standard, and had been built at some time in the late eighteenth century. It occupied an enviable position not far from the lazily flowing River Dissour, with Glenbower Wood's brooding mystery to its north and west, and glorious open countryside to the east. The enormous mass of the woods of Glenane and Glengarra lay to its north. Glenbower was the centre of the problem that urgently needed to be resolved.

As the people carrier drew into the lengthy driveway, it was greeted by a deafening cacophony of crow calls to welcome the saviour of all crow-kind to their neck of the woods.

Hugo looked over at Sean and they both smiled, knowing full well that the Boys in Black would be there to greet them.

"Well now," Seamus O'Croake said to the Grand Black Master of Cawk's Clan, who happened to be his brother from the same brood. He was called Fergal O'Croake. "Our saviour is here, and he is yooman as we foresaw all those years ago. A very young yooman

CHAPTER FOUR

in their way of counting, although that counts for nought in our terms."

"The question is, will this yooman be up to the challenge?" Fergal asked pointedly.

"He is the only yooman I have found that can communicate with our kind," Seamus replied sharply. "And what is more, he has a cousin with him who also understands us and our dilemma. Two equally clever yooman minds will be able to deal with those who would dare to destroy Glenane and Glenbower, our homelands for hundreds of yooman years."

"But that's not all, is it brother?" Fergal interrupted. "The second, even more disastrous phase would be to let the yoomans divert our great River Dissour, allowing its flood plains to be drained. This would enable them to build hundreds *more* yooman nesting sites where their ugly dwelling places might grow."

"The young yooman's last words to me were to consider bringing back some of our wonderful country's legends to help with the fight," Seamus O'Croake explained. "Just what he – they – have in mind, I do not know."

"Then we must ask them," his brother Fergal O'Croake insisted. "It is *our* land and *our* homes that are in danger."

-o-

"What's going to be our first move?" Sean asked Hugo over breakfast early the following day while everyone else was still in bed.

"Perhaps we ought to visit the scene of the council's potential crime?" Hugo replied with a smile, after another mouthful of toast and orange marmalade.

"How do you mean?" Sean said, only half sure what his cousin was saying. "You don't mean … the wood?"

"Indeed," Hugo agreed. "I feel sure Mr Seamus O'Croake and his boys will be there. Don't you?"

They ate and drank in silence, not wishing to disturb anyone else before they left to find their way to the river close by, and then north and west to the wood.

"Good morning, boys," a soft female voice surprised them as they ate.

"Granny … and Gramps!" they exclaimed, turning round sharply to see their grandparents. "How—?"

"We are always up early, little ones," Essie replied. "As we know where you are heading and how long you will be gone, you will find a few sandwiches, a flask of tea – because I know you both like tea – two jam tarts and a bottle of lemonade in those rucksacks by the outside door. Just to put you on until you have finished your … business."

"Thank you, Granny," Hugo said as he hugged her.

"From the bottom of our stomachs!" Sean added with a chortle, joining in eagerly.

"You'd better be on your way before everyone else gets up and delays your start," Grandpa Shylock advised. "You know what your sisters are like."

The two boys finished their breakfast, packed their things and headed for the back gate to Grandpa's back garden. This led to a footpath which took them to the river and ultimately to the wood, where they were sure they would have a significant welcome from the Boys in Black.

Although Sean and Hugo appeared outwardly calm, they were both beginning to feel their excitement building as they neared the river.

CHAPTER FOUR

"Well, good morning, Sean O'Keefe and Hugo Mayes," a raucously edgy caw greeted them as they approached the outer reaches of Glenbower Wood, with its dark, mysterious depths stretching beyond. "May I introduce you to my blood brother, Fergal O'Croake, the Grand Black Master of Cawk's Clan?"

"Pleased to meet you both," Hugo replied, as he bowed his head briefly in recognition of Fergal O'Croake's important position.

"What do we need to know about this most serious of circumstances?" Sean asked gravely. "And how would you wish us to proceed?"

"The choice of how to proceed is yours entirely, Masters Hugo and Sean," Fergal O'Croake replied slowly. "But the situation is unbelievably dire. If the local council's development people continue with their present plan, it will mean the total destruction of our entire habitat and the loss of many of our clan, both present and future."

"Has representation been made to them?" Hugo asked, though he realised his cousin would probably have more detailed information about that.

"Local people have protested," Sean explained, turning to his cousin, "but to no avail. Their protests have fallen on deaf ears so far. It seems that if permission is granted to local builders, the council's powers-that-be stand to make a lot of money that will fill their own pockets."

"Ah!" Hugo whistled softly. "Then we need to take extraordinary steps by calling for help from extraordinary people."

"What do you mean?" Seamus O'Croake asked, a puzzled look crossing his normally expressionless face.

"Sean and I will talk it through tonight and formulate a plan that we will bring to you tomorrow," Hugo said calmly and quietly.

Chapter 5

"Did you feel and hear that?" Hugo gasped quietly, beckoning his cousin to be quiet and to stand still.

"A slight tingly feeling and a faint buzzing sound?" Sean replied.

As they halted their tracks by the bubbling river, Hugo's cheek began to tickle slightly as if—

"Be very still, Cousin," Sean warned in a hoarse whisper. "A beautiful butterfly just landed on your cheek. She seems to be trying to communicate with your about … something."

At that moment, everything stopped. The river stayed its lazy course, the breeze-disturbed trees were stilled, all bird sound ceased – everything except for Sean and Hugo and … Psyche, the beautiful tortoiseshell butterfly.

"Be warned," she whispered. "Once you decide to tread the path to the Other World in order to summon legendary creatures to support your cause, as I know you will, be aware that you may not be able to halt their onward march, although your objectives may be achieved. Be warned."

With that, she disappeared and life started to move again, slowly at first, as if nothing had happened and then on into real time.

"Interesting," Hugo muttered as they trudged back to Granny's place, having consumed all she had packed for them, although they had no idea when, or what it tasted like.

"Shall you?" Sean asked slowly, not really sure what his answer might be. "Do what Psyche said to you, that is?"

"Certainly, *we* will," Hugo replied, waiting for his cousin's response to his offer.

"Good oh!" his cousin agreed, grinning hugely. "Talk about our plans later?"

Their walk back to Granny and Grandpa's house took longer than expected. They were stopped several times by an unseen barrier that wouldn't allow them to move either forward or backwards until they had listened each time to some disembodied voice telling them what to expect should they return to this place and time.

Sean was convinced that these different voices were warning them not to come back, and that they were too young and too weak to succeed. On the contrary, Hugo felt they *were* being warned but only because they were in the right; they were strong enough to persuade unseen powers to revisit this world to right an impending wrong before it affected all the Irish crows he now called friends.

As they approached the wood's eaves they were stopped again by a large, sinister-looking hooded crow perched on a stout branch that barred the narrow path close to the riverbank. A darkening mist had gathered, cutting off all sight and sound except of the bird – and *she* was staring keenly at them.

Not one to be put off by a look, Hugo stepped forward towards the creature. Planting his feet firmly on the pebbly bank, he said, "Mistress Crow, it is good to meet you but nothing you may say or do will divert us from our chosen path."

"Are you not afraid?" the crow answered. "Do you not know who I am?"

"As I am from this land and understand its myths and folklore, I believe you are Badb Catha," Sean replied unabashed. "The goddess of war and harbinger of doom often takes the form of a hooded crow. We have been summoned to set right an impending wrong that the council folk of Cawk are about to visit on your brethren – our friends – the crows of Glenbower."

CHAPTER FIVE

"As the appointed one with ancestry in this area, I have the right to call upon the Ancients from Irish folklore to help us in our rightful quest," Hugo added.

"You are brave young men, undaunted by the powers you seek to unleash," Badb Catha replied. "I have to warn you, however, that even if you succeed in your rightful quest you may not survive the encounter."

"We'll deal with that when we are confronted by it," Hugo insisted, as he and Sean turned to each other.

When they looked back, the crow and branches were no longer there and they were heading up the garden path towards Granny's back door.

-o-

"Where have you two been?" Betsy asked, dancing about impatiently. "We've been looking everywhere for you!"

"Hopefully trying to put right an outrageous wrong," Hugo replied calmly, as he sat by the roaring fire that never seemed to go out. "Granny Essie, the feast you made for us was excellent, wasn't it, Sean?" He turned to his cousin, eyebrows raised, seeking his support. He did this because neither of them could remember *when* they ate or, in fact, *what* they ate.

"We met one or two interesting characters along the way and saw some astounding scenery down by the river," Sean replied, equally calmly. "As Cousin Hugo said, Granny, lunch was delicious. Loved the corned beef sandwiches … and the tea, of course."

An almost imperceptible frown wandered across Hugo's brow as he turned towards his cousin, whose face bore a slightly self-satisfied smile. Sean's guess most definitely had hit the mark.

"When do we get to go down to the woods to stroll along the river?" Mandy complained as they sat at the table for tea.

"Let's be real, Mandy," Sean scoffed. "When was the last time you 'strolled' anywhere?"

"You are free to stroll whenever and wherever you want," Hugo added almost absent-mindedly, eyeing the huge cottage pie in the middle of the table, the cheesy topping still bubbling as its gorgeously tempting aroma filled the room.

"Shall we rush through the woods tomorrow then?" Betsy butted in sarcastically. "Or will you two be spending all of your time together on your own? If we are not to spend *any* time together – the four of us – we'll just ask Granny Essie and Grandpa Shylock to take us for a nice ride out … without you."

Sean and Hugo exchanged glances and almost silent sighs as they resigned themselves to spending time with their sisters.

"Sean?" his mother Judith said in support of the girls' wishes. Hugo's mum Gwen echoed her sister-in-law's sentiment.

"OK," the lads agreed. "We'll be revisiting the river flowing through Glenbower Wood in the afternoon because I believe our parents are going to find out details from local council at the offices in Cawk."

"Well, actually, no," Grandpa Shylock interrupted. "I have friends in reasonably high places there, so I'll be telephoning them to see how the land lies. Would that be all right, boys?"

"Thank you, Grandpa," Hugo added quietly. "But will that be enough? I mean—"

"Perfectly adequate," Granny Essie assured them. "Your grandpa used to be the top man there. So, if anyone is able to bring any weight to bear, it's him."

-o-

"This is exciting!" Betsy said to her cousin Mandy as they giggled and skipped around each other.

CHAPTER FIVE

The lazy river eddied and sauntered along around mini islands of lush reed beds and through tree roots that felt the limpid waters tentatively swish slowly around them. In places the waters narrowed enough to allow tree branches on opposite banks to touch in their attempts to bridge the narrows. All this the girls absorbed in awed wonder, never having experienced it before.

"Ouch! Wow!" The girls winced as they felt something sharp course through their bodies.

"What was *that*?" Mandy gasped, grimacing at the very mild sensation she had just experienced.

"Don't know, but I didn't like it," Betsy replied, none too pleased to have been 'attacked' without warning.

"Don't be so soft!" Sean scoffed. "A slight case of static electricity, that's all."

"We experienced that the last time we were here," Hugo agreed with his cousin, a vaguely mocking smile creasing his face. "It won't do any lasting damage, I can assure you."

They scrambled through a dense thicket of close-growing thorny bushes, heading back towards the river they had just left, expecting to catch sight of herons fishing in the shallows under the opposite bank close to a hefty clump of reeds. As they freed themselves from the grasping thorns, they stopped. The boys looked at each other, unable to believe what they were seeing.

The river had disappeared and they were standing on the crown of a wooded hill which looked over a valley with two lakes whose backdrop was Glendalough and the Wicklow Mountains.

A thin sliver of smoke spiralled lazily upwards from the chimney of a primitive-looking hut, outside of which sat a dishevelled person.

"See that man down there?" Sean said, pointing at the figure. "I believe he's a hermit."

"How do you know it's a man?" Mandy asked pointedly, following her brother's statement.

"I don't know many women who could wear such a long beard," Sean replied sarcastically. "It has to be male."

"But how did we get here?" Betsy asked, perplexed they had lost their way. "I thought we were supposed to be following the river."

"We were," Hugo insisted. "This isn't where we were supposed to be. Somehow I don't think we're anywhere near where we should be. Something's afoot that doesn't add up. I think we are in a countryside that we couldn't possibly have reached on foot. We're lost, I'm afraid."

Chapter 6

"Probably a good idea to sit down in front of this spectacular view and eat the packed lunch Granny Essie has provided," Hugo offered.

"I'm up for that," Sean agreed eagerly. "I think it would be good if Mandy and I had what's in *my* rucksack, and—"

"*We'll* have what's in ours," Hugo continued.

"Agreed!" they both exclaimed loudly, to be met by a returning echo a second or so later.

"And what if Betsy and I don't like what's in *either* bag?" Mandy asked rhetorically, to her cousin's vigorous nodding.

"Then how about if you nip down to the valley and knock on the door of what looks like a hermit's cottage down there?" Hugo replied sharply.

"Do you know, Hugo old chap, that this land is beginning to have an effect on you?" Sean asked with a sage nod of his head.

"How do you mean?" his cousin replied, not sure what he was saying.

"I do believe you are growing a sense of humour," Sean chortled, encouraging Hugo to chuckle back.

The more they sat and dined, the more they felt at peace. The glorious vista unfurling before them made them feel that everything might just turn out well.

"Do we have a problem here, Masters Hugo and Sean?" A gruff, raucous caw drifted down from the lower branches of a mature sessile oak tree.

"We were a little puzzled by the disappearance of the river we were following from Granny and Grandpa's house near Killeagh, Mr Seamus O'Croake," Hugo replied.

"The twice-wetted River Dissour disappeared because the magic of the woods brought you here to find answers," the crow said. "Close by, you will find Cloughlowrish Stone, sometimes called 'the listening stone', where no falsehood may be told. Speak your truth and what you ask will be granted."

"How about your friends carrying us back to Killeagh?" Betsy complained. She was not as happy as her brother and Cousin Sean seemed to be.

"What is likely to happen if we speak to the stone?" Hugo asked, liking the sound of the crow's wisdom.

"It is said that the giants Fionn mac Cumhaill and his Scottish adversary Parrah Boug McShagean will rise from Proleek and heed your request," Seamus O'Croake said, as he took off to re-join his people. "Speak wisely, but take care what you ask for. It may come back to bite you if you get it wrong."

"Well, Mandy and I want to go back to Granny and Grandpa's," Betsy complained. "It's getting chilly and we are hungry."

"You can't be!" Sean gasped. "We had only just finished our excellent feast when Seamus O'Croake arrive on the scene. Have you got worms or something?"

"This is probably our one chance to see and speak to the stone," Hugo urged his companions, knowing that Sean at least would be with him. "If we go back now, we might as well give up our quest and go back to England."

"And I suppose you will need a little help in your quest, young yoomans?" a raucous voice interrupted them again.

CHAPTER SIX

"Unless you can arrange a flypast of Air Force Chinooks, Mr O'Croake, I can't see how you could help," Hugo replied as he turned to face their friendly crow.

"Well, young man, that is where you could be mightily surprised," the crow began to explain with a cackle and a caw as he clicked his claws on the large flat-topped rock next to where they were sitting.

"If you have a way this … this quest can be sorted out quickly, Mr Crow, then I for one should like to hear it," Betsy added a little sharply. "Then perhaps we might be able to get back to Granny Essie's. I'm rather tired of all … this."

"All right, young lady," Seamus O'Croake suggested with a clack of his beak and a jiggling of his feet. "All of you stand together in the middle of this clearing and link arms tightly. Whatever you feel, do not let go of each other. Understand?"

"What's going to happen?" Mandy asked, more than a little concerned. "Where are we going?"

"We are going to help you conclude your quest by finding the Listening Stone," the crow croaked.

The four youngsters remained sitting in complete silence, looking at each other, not knowing what to say.

"If you mean to go, you should do as I ask and do it now," Mr O'Croake urged. "Otherwise you may as well—"

"Come on, you three!" Hugo ordered as he jumped to his feet. "Together. Quickly. Link arms."

Following his lead, they locked arms and waited. They became aware of O'Croake's flock raising an almighty commotion as it lifted into the air as one, slowly at first but then circling the children at the same time and the same speed. The faster they flew, the louder they became, until all the children could see was complete blackness, as if they were inside a darkly spinning top.

As the crow whirlwind reached its crescendo, their eyes closed automatically and they knew no more.

-o-

They awoke to an eerie silence and a half-light that disorientated them completely. The landscape had changed significantly. They were in open countryside, sitting with their backs resting against a smooth, blemish-free ancient rock that some distant ice age had no doubt deposited there umpteen thousands of years before. The crows had disappeared and left no sign that they had ever been there.

"How did we get here?" Betsy asked, nonplussed by the stark change in the terrain. "And where are the Boys in Black?"

"Does anyone else feel the gentle thrumming of this rock?" Mandy added. "Or is it me?"

"If you look at the dark-brown moss growing in patches on its face, you'll notice a gentle vibration which moves its tiny hair-like follicles," Hugo pointed out. "Most odd, and something I've never seen before."

"Listen very carefully," Sean advised, his ear flattened against its cool surface. "It's as if it's recording what we are saying and quietly playing our words back to us. Strange."

A look almost of shock flicked across Betsy's face as she pressed her ear to this unexpected recorder, to be followed immediately by a deep sigh and a gentle smile. "It seems to be talking to me!" she gasped. "*Not* repeating, but having a conversation. Talk to it, Hugo. Ask it what you want to know. I think it's been expecting us … for some time."

Chapter 7

"But it's gone four, and there's still no sign of them!" Mother Gwen and Aunt Judith reiterated – for the third time. "Where can they be, and what on earth must they be doing?"

"Stop worrying, you two!" Grandpa Shylock said. "It's very safe around here, and they'll be having … fun. Children never seem able to have fun these days, unlike in my day."

"But your day, Dad, was before time, rules and laws were invented," Uncle Michael scoffed, causing Cousin Josiah to guffaw loudly. "Way back in the Dark Ages."

"It's all right you laughing, youngster, but it comes to everybody sooner or later," Gramps replied sharply. "If you understand what to expect, then you'll be fine."

"Cup of tea and a slice of lemon drizzle cake anyone?" Granny Essie asked lightly, poking her head around the kitchen door.

"Yes, please!" Josiah agreed, jumping in quickly.

"Me too, please," Michael added, a flash of anticipation glinting in his eyes, not wanting to be left out. Granny Essie's cakes were legendarily exquisite, and nobody who was of sound mind ever refused.

-o-

"Could you speak a little louder, please?" Hugo asked politely, his ear pressed against the smooth ice-age rock. "We all need to be able to listen and join in."

"I can't hear anything," Mandy complained.

"Perhaps we need to leave communication to either Sean or Hugo, seeing as we all can't join in," Betsy butted in. This negotiating lark wasn't really her thing.

"I vote for Hugo," Sean agreed. "He knows better than I do how things need to be handled. What is more, he has real two-way discussions with Seamus O'Croake, and is likely to do the same here, too."

"I've already shared our concerns and wishes," Hugo informed his family. "I believe that we will receive some sort of an answer soon, although I don't know how soon that will be. We just have to be patient … and … wait."

"You speak with honesty and honour, Hugo Crow Master." A faint but deeply resonant disembodied voice rose from the rock almost immediately. "We are prepared to advise, and yet to warn." After a moment's pause, the voice went on, "The powers and legends you need to unleash to further your quest were born out of the bowels of this magnificent land in days long ago. Use them wisely."

"And the warning?" Hugo asked tentatively.

"Do not request more assistance than you need," the voice continued, "lest the powers unleashed may not be recalled."

The voice spoke no more.

"What does that all mean?" Betsy asked, as puzzled as ever.

"If we ask for support from these dormant powers, we have to be exact in what we ask for – and from whom," Hugo explained. "We must request no more than we need."

"And if we do?" Mandy said, as puzzled as her cousin Betsy.

"Then we release powers beyond belief on an unsuspecting world," Hugo added. "*That* could lead to disaster."

"What are these 'powers' you are talking about, then?" Betsy asked, almost disbelieving what all this was about. She wasn't too sure really, because she knew her brother of old. Talk about serious! Yet he had his good, kind and thoughtful side, as well as

CHAPTER SEVEN

being single-minded and forthright. He was, after all, born under the sign of Capricorn, and they are usually difficult to understand and get on with.

"The likes of Giant Fionn mac Cumhaill and his Scottish adversary, Giant Darrah Boug McShagean," Hugo offered in an awed voice.

"The first one is also known as Finn MacCool," Sean butted in proudly. "He's the one who fashioned the Giant's Causeway on the coast of County Antrim in the north during his battles with his Scottish adversary."

"There's no such thing as giants!" Betsy harrumphed loudly. "All stories and nonsense! Aren't they?"

With all this talk of folk lore and fantastic tales, the two girls weren't at all sure what was true and what was a fairy story. But Sean and Hugo knew, because they … believed.

"We have to be careful," Hugo warned, ignoring his sister's criticisms about *their* beliefs. "We must use our giants only as a threat. If we go too far, who knows what they will do and what they might destroy as they pound about in anger?"

"But how will we get the councillors to listen and cancel their silly, dangerous plans for Glenbower Wood?" Sean asked seriously.

"We ask some of our other 'contacts' to put a word in on our behalf, I think," Hugo added, a giant grin indicating his thoughts.

"Such as Badb Catha, do you think?" Sean giggled giddily.

"Who's Baddy Cathy when she's at home?" Mandy asked, not believing the half of it.

"She's the Goddess of War who took the form of a hooded crow a short while ago when Hugo and I took our first walk into the forest," Sean explained. "*She* stopped us in our tracks just by being … there. She was the one to give us our first warning."

"I believe she would be ideal as one of our first warners," Hugo suggested, causing his sister to frown because she didn't understand. "To be followed by the Morrighan, who…"

"Also appears as a crow or raven," Sean added quickly with a chortle.

"Stop! Stop!" the girls yelled.

"For goodness' sake!' Betsy groaned loudly. "Can't do with all this childish, made-up stuff. You've gone too far, and—"

"Too far, you say?" a menacing, velvety, female voice interrupted the young human. Betsy's tongue froze to the roof of her mouth while her feet were fixed to the ground so she couldn't move.

Mandy and the boys turned towards the voice and saw a large shiny-black raven perching on a thick oak branch level with their heads.

"You are Morrighana Macha, the Goddess of War, sister to Badb Catha who we have met already," Hugo said, matter of factly. "We are glad to see you."

"Your proposition intrigues and puzzles me – to an extent," the raven said, fixing her gaze on him. Taken aback that she was unable to exert her influence over him, she tried to see into his mind but met with failure. "You are—"

"Impervious to your control tricks?" Hugo replied. His benign smile disconcerted her.

Almost imperceptibly, the raven disappeared and a beautiful, imperious young woman with long shiny-black hair, dark eyes and flowing black clothing and a cloak made her way slowly through the trees.

"At last we meet, Master Hugo," Morrighana said, as Betsy regained her faculties and Mandy closed her jaw, which had been

CHAPTER SEVEN

resting on her chest from shock and awe. "This meeting has been a long time coming."

"Indeed it has, Morrighana Macha," Hugo said quietly, exciting extreme wonder in the eyes and minds of his sibling and his cousins.

Betsy could not understand how little she knew about her twin, the person she should know almost as well as she knew herself. In fact, she was so shocked by all of this that she wasn't sure if indeed they had been born from the same mother!

"You obviously have a serious agenda, Master Hugo," Morrighana said. "Pray explain what it is, and how I may fit in to this 'agenda'?"

"You probably are not aware that local grandees are about to wipe Glenbower and Glenane Woods from the face of the earth," Hugo explained. "They are also about to divert and drain the River Dissour."

"Their reason for this?" she replied, almost *too* calmly in the circumstances.

"To provide hundreds, or even thousands, of new houses for people that don't belong here. That will destroy the habitat for thousands of creatures," Sean interrupted.

"Such an act would also dispossess thousands of your adopted creatures – the crows that have called those woods home for hundreds of years," Hugo added. "We would like you to help 'persuade' these people of the wrongness of this action."

"And how would you suggest I go about this 'persuasion'?" Morrighana asked, although she no doubt knew where she might start.

"You, My Lady, are the Goddess of War, Battle and Strife," Hugo pointed out. "The one ingredient in all of those is the effect of fear on the individual. I am sure you must have limitless ways of instilling enough fear into their quiet and miserable lives to make them wish to withdraw such a selfish and destructive action."

"I must admit that frightening unimportant little yoomans, sometimes to death, can be fun," Morrighana said with a smile. "I am sure, too, that I know of several like-minded individuals who might wish to lend a helping hand in this 'quest' of yours."

"Excellent!" Hugo said, punching the air in triumph. "I am your servant, My Lady."

"Really?" she replied quickly, her eyes flashing with excitement, as she rubbed her hands together in anticipation.

"Simply a figure of speech," Hugo added, not wishing Morrighana Macha to run away with the wrong idea.

"So, who will you invite along to help?" Sean asked. "A banshee or two, maybe? Or even … or even the Hag of Beara, perhaps?"

Turning back from grinning at his cousin, Sean realised that Morrighana was no longer there. There was only the vaguest of down draughts from the wings of some large bird to remind them of what they had just witnessed.

They had turned away from the Listening Stone to trudge back for tea when Betsy said, with a significantly shocked tone to her voice, "Do you see what I see? That's impossible, surely."

Not forty yards away, across a familiar field, stood Hugo and Betsy's mum. They were standing behind the gate leading into Granny and Grandpa's back garden.

"But … that's … not … possible," Mandy gasped slowly. "We've only just set off!"

The girls turned to Hugo to see if he might have an explanation. "Some things we *don't* understand," he said quietly. "But, conveniently, we can call them … magic."

Chapter 8

"Something you might like to know," Grandpa said as they sat down for breakfast the next day. "A meeting is to be held about the future of the woods and the river the day after tomorrow."

"We've only really got a couple of days to change their minds, then," Hugo said, a far-away look in his eyes as he started to work out how he could let Morrighana know.

"I've already made representations to the council, and this meeting has been scheduled hastily in response to my words," Grandpa replied. He nodded almost imperceptibly at the planning that he thought was taking shape in his grandson's head. "The main meeting will be several months away, so this one is for me."

"Any idea where this meeting will take place, Grandpa?" Hugo asked.

"In Glenbower Wood by the river bend," Shylock replied after a moment or two's pause while he enjoyed a mouthful of his favourite tea.

"Excellent!" Hugo thought with glee. This made organising his 'extra' help a whole lot easier. All he had to be concerned about now was how he would contact the Goddess of Strife, and whether she would deliver sufficient fear of retribution to the gathered councillors if they didn't listen to reasoned argument about the sanctity of the wood and the life-giving river that coursed through it.

-o-

Grandpa's garden was lovely at this time of year. Large by any stretch of the imagination, it boasted several sessile oak and hazel trees, and holly bushes in abundance. It was easy to see that Granny Essie had had more than a passing hand in the garden's design and planting, as islands of astonishing colour burst upon the eye no matter where one looked.

Although this was the first time Hugo had stayed here in his few short years, it was a place he knew he could spend quiet time tussling with the many problems that had settled on his little shoulders. His parents and grandparents were well aware of the vast distance between his power of reasoning and his six years of age. Some people might call him 'babyish'. How little those people knew!

Sitting and thinking was what he liked to do best, while his Cousin Sean played kick-ups with his football and the girls played on the swings down by the bottom fence. They also loved to play with their dolls near the sand pit not far from the waterfall, which briefly interrupted the lively stream's charge before it buried itself under the fence as it sought the River Dissour and the wider sea beyond.

"Thinking, little master?" a gruff voice drew his attention to a familiar low oak branch nearby.

"Mr Seamus O'Croake!" Hugo greeted his friendly crow with a cheery smile. "Just the person I need to see." He explained briefly what his grandpa had said to him about the meeting, and what had happened when they had met Morrighana the day before.

O'Croake let out a loud caw when he understood what Hugo had done. "You realise that she will carry out any promise she has made to you?" the crow explained.

"But she didn't promise *anything*," Hugo replied. "She simply … disappeared."

"That's enough for her," the crow went on. "If she wasn't going to intervene, she would have disappeared immediately without giving you a hearing. She is intrigued by the fact that she has failed

CHAPTER EIGHT

to control *you* as she has done with most other yoomans. It was obviously also a shock to her that you are so young."

"Will you – can you – contact her with the details so she can—?" Hugo started.

"Yes, I can and will do as you ask, but she will already know," O'Croake replied. "I imagine she will have decided what's going to happen. The one thing we cannot guarantee is that she will not cause irreparable damage to any of her audience. Beggars can't be choosers in cases like this, though."

With that, he lifted his aged body slowly into the air, shoulders hunched and feet trailing behind, almost like a heron in full, glorious flight.

"Was that Mr Crow?" Betsy asked as she approached her brother, her doll's body in one hand and its head in the other. "Can you mend my Jessie, please? Of course, you can't because you're only my age, and we can't—"

As she was talking, Hugo took both head and body from her, snapped them back into place and returned it to her in seconds.

"How did you do that?" she whooped, clutching Jessie to her chest. "You're not supposed to be able to do that. You're younger than me, for goodness' sake!"

"Only by a minute, dear sister," Hugo replied simply. "I can use logic, too. Our business here should be finished within the next few days, then we can play as you've been wanting to since we arrived. I'm sorry I have been busy, but we have to stop the desolation that *will* be caused if the councillors don't change their minds."

"Do you see that glorious oak tree over there, growing through the yew hedge not far from the gate into the field?" Sean asked his cousin as he nudged him in the ribs. "The one that looks like an enormous galleon in full green sail?"

"Do you mean the one with a raven sitting next to a crow at the end of that leaf-free branch?" Hugo replied. "The ones that seem to be having an earnest conversation?"

"Mm," Sean muttered. "Are you thinking the same as me? We know crows can do this, but different corvids … together? Not sure about that."

"What have we seen lately that bears some resemblance to what we're seeing now?" Hugo asked. "Badb and Morrighana, perhaps?"

"Never thought of that. Yes, of course!" Sean answered as he turned to his cousin.

"Gone!" Hugo muttered, surprised.

"Flown off together, eh?" Sean said with a wry smile.

"No," Hugo said quite emphatically. "Just … gone. Disappeared without trace."

Chapter 9

"I think we could be in for a dose of trouble," the local council clerk Mr O'Dourves muttered, his mouth full of chocolate biscuit and café latte. Until recently he had been a chef at The Square Chair restaurant in Cawk, but had decided on a change of career. Politics had seemed to be a more productive – and easier – path to tread.

"How do you mean?" his assistant Mr O'Driscoll asked, puzzled by the reference.

"Do you remember Shylock O'Keefe?" Mr O'Dourves went on. "Top chap who used to run the show here? Had a lot of clout in many high circles?"

"*That* Shylock O'Keefe?" O'Driscoll gasped. "They used to call him the Smiling Assassin, if memory serves.'

"I remember that only too well." Mr O'Dourves shuddered and wiped his already perspiring shiny bald head. "He had a habit of telling you what he thought of your inadequacies with a smile on his face. Ouch!"

"So, what about him?" O'Driscoll asked. "You said you thought we might be in for a dose of trouble. And?"

"Well, you remember the O'Sly family that wanted to purchase a small part of Glenbower Wood for, er, redevelopment?" O'Dourves said.

"Small part? Redevelopment?" O'Driscoll scoffed loudly. "Try … 'all of the wood and replace it with several hundred houses – *expensive* houses'. How can Shylock cause us trouble when he's retired and he doesn't know about our *other* business?"

"Don't you believe it!" O'Dourves insisted sharply. "He has always known … everything. I bet he even knows how much the O'Slys are paying for the Wood, how much the wood from the

Wood is being sold for, and how much is going to the council. Catch my drift?"

"Of course I do, but what can he do about it when he doesn't have any *EVIDENCE*?" O'Driscoll hissed, putting a heavy emphasis on his last word with a sly grin on his devious face. "You worry too much. There is nothing on this Earth he can bring to bear either to persuade you to change your mind or to use against you in a court of law in this fair land."

"It's not a court of law that I'm afraid of," O'Dourves muttered as he finished his coffee and biscuit.

"Why on earth do you drink that muck?" his companion said forcefully. "You don't even like it!"

-o-

"Well, my lads, it seems that Mr O'Dourves has a lot to answer for in this matter," Grandpa O'Keefe said to his grandsons at dinner the day before the meeting was due to take place in Glenbower Wood.

"Is it what we thought, Grandpa?" Sean asked eagerly. Hugo also wanted to know how close they'd got.

"It seems that our friend the council clerk stands to 'earn' more money than you can shake a stick at from this illegal transaction," Grandpa Shylock replied slowly. "Although they know that I know what they are up to, they seem to be playing a waiting game."

"Waiting game, Grandpa?" Hugo asked, not sure what he meant by 'shaking a stick' either.

"They will be waiting to see if I react and, if I do, what form my reaction will take," Grandpa explained.

"Is the meeting still going ahead then?" Sean asked, wanting clarification so both he and Hugo might be prepared. "How much danger will there be to us?"

CHAPTER NINE

"None from the council," Grandpa assured them. "It all depends on what other forces are involved – and only you two know that. Are you prepared to pay the ultimate price, should it come to it?"

"Yes, Grandpa, we are," the boys replied firmly, looking at each other as they agreed with a nod.

"This is too important an issue to be worried about any outcome for us personally," Hugo added. "We are in this together and we will see it through together, no matter the consequence."

Sean nodded his head vigorously and punched the air. He looked around to see everyone tucking in to roast beef and Yorkshire pudding, with Granny's renowned roasted taties and a mountain of crispy veg you could almost climb physically. Granny Essie was a wonderful cook, no doubt about it.

They were taking things slowly and easily because they had glimpsed the most enormous bowl of trifle on a ridiculously small table close to the kitchen door. They *had* to find room for a dish or five of that!

-o-

"What is to happen tomorrow then, Mr Seamus O'Croake?" his brother Grand Master Fergal asked as they flew in to roost in the clan's favourite sleeping trees in Glenbower Wood, from where they could keep a watch.

"Not too sure, as you might expect, Brother," Seamus replied, once he had settled. "Yoomans aren't like us, you know. We make a decision and stick to it, whereas yoomans can change their minds and throw all previous decisions through their windows with no notice at all. They then blame either changing circumstances or further information that has just come to light."

"Meeting place time?" Fergal asked.

"As it's a full moon tonight, the meeting will have to be early evening to get even closer to the deadline," Seamus answered. "The problem might be the other condition for solving the problem."

"Which is?" his brother asked, more than a little puzzled at this 'small' conundrum.

"For the agreement to be binding, it has to be sworn in the middle of Glenbower Wood, the seat of our ancestry and the centre of our dilemma," Seamus explained. "But I've no doubt the 'extra' support our young yooman, Hugo Mayes, gives us will help with that issue."

"And how do you know that?" his brother scoffed, unconvinced.

"It's a feeling I have in my bones," Seamus insisted quietly. "*Those* feelings have never let me down before, and there's no reason to think they will tomorrow. Sleep now, my brother, and we will see what tomorrow brings."

-o-

Hugo slept deeply until the early hours of the morning in the room he shared with his cousin Sean. They were kindred spirits right enough, and it was only the year difference in age – and birth, of course – that stopped them being twins. They often spoke about living closer together so they might share more excitement and adventure.

Unfortunately, Hugo's parents and Aunt Judith and Uncle Michael were not about to trade homes and countries to allow them to do that. They would just have to spend more holiday time in each other's company.

Fortunately, Betsy and Mandy were also very much alike while being poles apart from their respective brothers. Both sets of parents said often that it wouldn't be a good idea to have children

CHAPTER NINE

with the same personality and character in the same family. How wrong they were!

"You still asleep?" Sean asked his cousin quietly, so as not to disturb him if he was.

"Been awake for an hour or so," Hugo answered quietly, too.

"Me too," Sean agreed. "Thinking through today's test?"

"Indeed," his cousin muttered. "I would certainly like to know two things: how are we going to get the council representatives into the heart of the wood, and how are we to arrange a full moon?"

"I think we'll have to leave that to one of the characters we've already spoken to," Sean suggested. "I have no doubt that everything will sort itself out in the end. According to Grandpa's charts, tonight is *supposed* to have a full moon."

"Then we'll have to trust to chance," Hugo said, as he settled down again.

This was going to be a long day, and everything they had worked towards *had* to fall into place. No use being worried about the outcome, they would just have to trust in…

The cousins fell asleep again at exactly the same time to allow their bodies to regenerate and to build their strength for what most definitely would be a mentally taxing and physically tiring day.

Chapter 10

Hugo often wondered about the purpose of dreams. Waking in the morning, there was always the vaguest remnant of … something at the back of his mind that told him he had been part of a strangely disturbing event. Whatever he did to cast back his mind to find out what it was, only tantalising scraps that meant nothing remained and even they disappeared very quickly. This night, however, was very different.

Everything that had happened over the last day or two swam into sharp focus, telling him what had happened, why it had happened, and what he should do not to lose his grasp on what the outcome had to be.

He awoke at dawn, just as the local bird chorus was getting into full swing, with all that was to happen this day clear in his mind. Unusually, his cousin Sean was still asleep, undisturbed by the dreams that had drawn in Hugo and woken him up.

"Busy day today, my lad," Granny Essie said as she watched him eat his breakfast. "You look as if you know the outcome of today's events already."

"I do, Granny," he replied calmly. "At least, I think I do. But I've a feeling Mr O'Dourves and Mr O'Driscoll might have something up their sleeves other than their arms that might get them out of this quandary. I had a dream – a very clear dream – that showed me several possible ways things might go, and only one of them was positive."

"Dreams are notoriously tricksy because they are based on nothing substantial," Essie said. "They could mean anything you want them to mean, and no-one would be any the wiser."

"Hold on, my good fellow." Sean's voice accosted him from the door into the hallway. "Not thinking of going anywhere without me, I trust?"

"Certainly not," Hugo harrumphed, indignantly. "Just having a leisurely breakfast and a chat with Granny. You're late up. Slept too well?"

"Slept like a dream but, unusually, wasn't disturbed by any of those," Sean said as he waited for his toast and tea. "You?"

Hugo explained his experiences in the night as he devoured his toast and honey. Unabashed, he had set to again, not wanting his friend to feel alone in breakfasting. You just couldn't beat lashings of granary bread toasted to within an inch of its life, washed down by your favourite tea – enough to feed a growing body!

"Are we doing anything exciting today?" Betsy and Mandy asked as they danced into the room.

"Something that doesn't involve walking, and talking about silly trees and birds and … people," Mandy added as she skipped to the table with a twirl or two before she sat down.

"Do you know, Mandy, you make me feel giddy with all your twirls and skipping and stuff that normal people don't do," Sean gasped as he refilled his and Hugo's mugs.

"Well, you're so stuffy and boring sometimes, Sean O'Keefe," Mandy said dismissively. "Is there nothing else we can do that doesn't involve black birds?"

"It may be boring for you, but this affair is very important for the woods and the crows and all the other wild creatures that live in it," Hugo explained gently. "If we let these council people have their own way without redress, the whole area will be changed forever. We can't let them get away with it."

CHAPTER TEN

"Boring!" Betsy sighed as she dropped her shoulders in frustration. "So, what are we going to do today, then?"

"We – Sean and I – will be doing our research in readiness for this evening's meeting to—" Hugo tried to explain, which was incredibly difficult to do with such excitable and easily distracted girls whose minds regularly flitted from place to place.

"Who would like to come for a ride to Killeagh with me, Mummy Gwen and Mummy Judith?" Granny Essie asked.

"Is Gramps coming too?" Betsy asked eagerly.

"No," Granny Essie replied. "He's staying here. He has some very important business to attend to."

"Are we going by bus then, Granny?" Mandy said, a little puzzled because Grandpa *always* drove wherever they went.

"No," Granny Essie replied again. "*I* will be driving."

"*You*, Granny?" the two girls gasped incredulously. "But—"

"Before you die from shock, I'll tell you that I've been driving *longer* than your grandpa," she replied with a smile. "I used to drive a taxi *and* a passenger coach for a living until only two years ago, and—"

"Yay!" the girls whooped. "Then we'll come with you to Killeagh for morning coffee … and afternoon tea!"

-o-

"Now they're away to town, *we* need to be prepared for *our* adventure," Grandpa Shylock offered. "Your respective dads don't want to be involved, so it will be just the three of us."

"What time's the next meeting, Grandpa?" Sean asked, itching to get started. "And how are we going to get there?"

"Seeing as the meeting place has to be at the centre of Glenbower Wood by the River Dissour in the early evening, that's where we will be heading – on foot," Grandpa explained carefully.

"How will Mr O'Dourves and Mr O'Connell, together with their cronies, be 'encouraged' to meet us there?" Sean asked, with a slight inkling of what the answer might be.

"I think they will have no choice in the matter," Hugo replied with a nod and a wink. "I believe they will be there whether they like it or not."

Sean and Hugo went into an uncharacteristic giggling huddle to guess how the blow on the council men might fall. In this case, would they get their just desserts?

"Grandpa?" Hugo asked. "I once heard someone ask if the end justified the means. I didn't understand then what it meant, and I still don't."

"In a situation where a good outcome is very important, *any* way of achieving it – even a bad one – is acceptable," Grandpa explained. "In my view, usually it's not the right way to go about things. *This* case is different, however, because we need to impress upon these characters that they can't cause that sort of devastation just for money."

"We are not going to let that happen," Hugo insisted seriously. "I don't care about the money. I feel the crows' home and the habitat of all the other creatures that live in those woods is more important. Is it true that they have said the river can be diverted, too?"

"Yes, it is true," Grandpa agreed. "But that will never be allowed to happen. That one, fortunately, is a national issue and won't ever be agreed to. Cup of tea and a bite then, mi boyos, before we're away?" he suggested, much to their excitement and delight. "Looks like rain."

CHAPTER TEN

"But don't we need a clear full moon tonight?" Sean asked, a little taken aback.

"We do," Grandpa replied with a grin. "We also need to have patience. I can't see the weather is going to be an issue. It's blustery, so any rain will be short-lived. You both ready for this?"

"Certainly are! Too right!" they both insisted excitedly as they moved to the door.

"Then, let's away," Grandpa urged. "Tonight's the night for setting wrongs to right."

Chapter 11

The three travellers enjoyed the saunter through Grandpa and Granny's back garden, listening to the wonderful variety of joyous bird song from blackbird, thrush, robin, dunnock and a whole other range too numerous to mention.

"Can't hear our friendly Boys in Black," Sean remarked as they reached the latched gate at the end of the garden. He was more than a little puzzled by their omission. "They are always calling each other at this time of day, letting each other know that it will soon be time to retire to roost."

"I can hear the other corvids – raven, magpie, rook, jackdaw, hooded crow – but none of Mr Seamus O'Croake's clan," Hugo added. He didn't like even the smallest change in his everyday life, even if he had been warned about it beforehand. "Probably concerned what *could* happen this night."

"Very true." A raucous cawing call alerted him to the oak tree growing close by the eaves of Glenbower Wood. "What is going to happen this evening, Masters Hugo and Sean, to settle all future evenings? I see you have brought reinforcements. Good evening, Mr Shylock O'Keefe. It is a long while since we last held a meaningful conversation."

"Indeed it is, Mr O'Croake," Grandpa replied, to the surprise and shock of his grandsons. "It must be at least a year, but then at my age I don't seem to get out much any more."

The crow froze, his body still but his head moving slightly as he sniffed the air. He rolled his eyes and clicked his beak almost silently.

"I noticed, too, as we approached the wood, that all wild creature noise had ceased," Grandpa observed. "Do you have any idea why, my friend?"

"That I do not, Mr O'Keefe," the crow replied, dismayed that he could not even guess at the reason. "But it bodes ill for a good outcome for tonight's business. We are lacking even Mistress Moon, whom we need to validate our meeting with the reprobate council men, O'Dourves and O'Driscoll."

"And our 'special' guests?" Grandpa asked, wondering if Seamus O'Croake would understand his reference to the characters from Irish legend and folklore that could be taking part.

"As far as I am aware, some interesting witnesses might be putting in an appearance or two," the old crow replied as he took off. "See you all later."

Then he was gone. They were unable to see where he had gone because the gloaming was beginning to steal in on stealthily quiet feet. As the three travellers reached the appointed meeting place in the middle of the wood, the silvery moon crept out from behind a friendly cloud to announce that now was the time to account for past actions.

"I don't see the councillors," whispered Sean, disappointment in his voice and a sense of betrayal in his eyes.

Suddenly the clearing was bathed in eerie moonlight. Unexpectedly, at its centre, could be seen two very startled yooman grown-ups – Mr O'Dourves and Mr O'Driscoll. They looked at each other and around them, wondering how on earth they had been plucked from their comfortable evening at home and deposited, still in their carpet slippers, in the middle of a very spooky wooded clearing.

As the light waxed, there could be seen countless black shapes appearing out of the surrounding gloom to take up their grandstand places on oak and hazel branches to witness proceedings.

"Hello?" Mr O'Dourves called tentatively. "Anybody there?"

CHAPTER ELEVEN

Unexpectedly, a small boy entered the moonlit circle. He was unafraid of the hundreds of crows around him and definitely had no fear of the two adults facing him.

"What are you doing here, sonny?" O'Driscoll said, a mocking tone decorating his words. "Shouldn't you be at home in—?"

The young boy turned to face him, obliging him to stop talking with one steely look, rendering O'Driscoll's power of speech useless and his mind blank.

"You have been brought here to account for your illegal actions in allowing this ancient woodland to be sold, destroyed and built upon," the young boy accused O'Dourves. "What say you?"

"This is ridiculous," Mr O'Dourves protested, "and certainly none of your business."

"It is everyone's business," a sinister rasping voice threatened from the gloom beyond the circle of light. "As such, we will draw you to account this very night. If you do not withdraw the order – in writing – you will be destroyed."

"You can't hurt me," the council clerk sneered. "I have the law and the police force on my side, so you can't—"

His face dropped slowly as a terrifying female form, dressed entirely in severe black, grew out of the shadows. At the same time another figure, dressed in dark grey with fiery crimson streaks, grew out of the earth itself before their feet.

"If we can't persuade you that your disagreement will rain fire and damnation upon your heads, perhaps our two companions will," threatened Morrighana and Badb, goddesses of war and strife.

As the two yooman adults stood, unable to move or to speak, they felt the ground begin to shake as if several enormously heavy feet were walking towards them.

Rigid with untold fear, their eyes couldn't believe the two gigantic bodies that boomed into the Circle of Light. The two legendary mountainous giants – Fionn mac Sumhaill and his Scottish adversary, Parrah Boug McShagean – lumbered from the shadows, filling the Circle of Light entirely.

This was too much for O'Dourves and O'Driscoll. They turned to flee – but none of their muscles would function, rendering their legs and arms useless, their tongues still and their eyes unable to shut out the monstrous form of these two giants.

"Now, my little fellows," Fionn mac Sumhaill – otherwise known as Finn McCool – boomed. "What are we going to do with you? Maybe braised and served with dumplings? What do you say, Parrah?"

"Well," the Scottish giant replied, "I'm not particularly hungry yet as I've just eaten three spit-roasted pigs, fourteen loaves of granary bread and a complete tree of golden apples."

"Are you not feeling well, my worthy friend?" McCool said, a look of surprise in his mountainous face. "You usually consume much more than that!"

"Started my new diet the other day – sea food," the Scottish mountain replied. "But that doesn't contain more than one human a day."

"Sea food?" McCool sniggered. "What's that? See food and eat it?"

They both burst out laughing with an earth-shattering and forest-shaking guffaw that had all, including the crows, covering their ears.

"We give in," the two puny humans confessed weakly. "We'll sign any papers now. Just don't … eat us!"

CHAPTER ELEVEN

"Done!" Shylock O'Keefe shouted as he marched purposefully into the Circle of Light, followed by his two grandsons. "I happen to have the papers right here."

"Well, if it isn't my old friend, Shylock O'Keefe," the Irish giant boomed, kneeling and bending over to see him more clearly. "I thought it might have been you behind all of this."

"Actually, Old Chap, I had little to do with it," Grandpa O'Keefe explained at the top of his voice so the giant could hear. "My grandsons here are the main players and organisers in this wonderful event, along with Mr Seamus O'Croake, our estimable Master Crow."

As he spoke the leader of the crows alighted on Hugo's shoulder.

"We owe our homes and our families for generations to come to this young yooman and his cousin," O'Croake cawed. "Along with our undying gratitude. I propose that they are granted freedom of Glenbower Wood for as long as their families shall live."

A deafening cacophony of caws raced around the invisible circle in support of Seamus O'Croake's sentiment. Then all the crows lifted off as one and flew around the three travellers, saluting them with dipped wing tips as they flew off to roost.

"Did we actually really witness all that?" Sean asked, quite overwhelmed. "I mean, giants, goddesses and saluting crows?"

"Indeed, we did, my boy," Grandpa Shylock assured him. "Legend coming to life and folklore helping creatures in need, eh? It doesn't get much better than that."

"Thank you for all your help and support, Grandpa, when few would have believed let alone helped," Hugo said. "You made all the difference."

"Nay, Hugo," Grandpa replied. "*You* did all the work. All I did was put in a word here and there."

"How do you know Finn McCool, Grandpa?" Sean asked, a new look of awe and admiration lighting his face. "How cool was that!"

"Ha Ha!" Grandpa chortled. "I see what you did there!"

Unfortunately, Hugo's serious nature and questionable sense of humour didn't allow him to catch the funny his cousin had uttered.

"Did anyone see where our friendly giants and goddesses went?" Sean asked, looking about the empty, now shadowy circle of trees.

"More to the point, where are our two councillors?" Hugo noted.

"That, along with Finn McCool, is probably a story for another day," Grandpa Shylock assured them with a grin and raised eyebrows. "It's now time for bed. Anyone coming?"

The boys turned to follow their grandpa. As they reached the eaves of the circle of trees, they both felt a strong tingling sensation coursing through their bodies and heard a faint, distant cackling sound.

They slowed, looked at each other, shrugged, and headed for home.

Chapter 12

For once in his young life, Hugo wasn't up at the crack of dawn. This day was one of very few when he hadn't welcomed the new morning's dawn chorus of a myriad happy birds as they serenaded the world. By the time he *did* get up, the household had been functioning for quite some time, and the wildlife thereabouts had been managing to survive happily for several hours.

"Welcome to the land of the living, Brother," Betsy joked as he settled at the table for his breakfast.

"Have you eaten *already*, Sister?" he replied.

"Indeed, we all have," she said, "but I am sure we would all be happy to set to again. After all, it seems like an age since *we* ate last."

"You all right, my boy?" Grandpa Shylock asked, a little concerned that his grandson's lethargy might be due to illness.

"I *am*, Grandpa," Hugo replied. "I feel just a little bit tired after all we've been through over the last week. No more, no less."

"When are we going back home?" Betsy asked generally, to no-one in particular. "I've had a good time here with Mandy and Grandpa Shylock and Granny Essie. Oh, and Sean, of course. But it is time—"

"We are booked on the ferry from Rosslare to Fishguard reasonably early tomorrow afternoon, which will mean early to bed and early to rise," Mamma Gwen said. "Your Grandpa has agreed to take us to the port."

"Can't wait to try those donuts again!" Betsy said, rubbing her hands together in glee.

"We will be taking sandwiches and some of Granny's home baking, which is much better than donuts," Mamma explained. "Agreed?"

"All right," Betsy agreed reluctantly.

"If you don't like Granny's baking, I'll have yours as well as mine, and you can have … a donut," Hugo offered with a smile. "That works for me."

"It's all right, Brother dear," Betsy assured him. "I'll cope."

-o-

"So, what are you going to do when you get home, Hugo?" his cousin Sean asked as they enjoyed a kick around in the garden.

"Back to a normal life – whatever that is," Hugo replied. "I shall certainly miss *you*, old chap. This week has been excellent, don't you think?"

"It has been a worthwhile week for *us*, certainly." A raucous cawing sound assailed them from the top of the pergola close to the house.

"Good morning, Mr O'Croake," Hugo greeted the crow. "I am very glad we were able to help your worthy clan."

"Are you sure this is Mr Seamus O'Croake, the leader of the Boys in Black?" Sean asked in a whispered aside. "All I can hear is a cawing noise that all crows make."

"Please give your cousin Sean our grateful thanks. Once you have returned to your home, we will no longer communicate in yooman tongue," the crow warned. "Unfortunately, this episode has taught us not to trust yooman kind – with one or two exceptions, of course."

"Does that mean that you won't be returning with us?" Hugo asked, more than a little disconcerted and disappointed. "If that is

CHAPTER TWELVE

so, I shall miss our conversations because I, too, am learning not to trust everyone … entirely."

"We will remain here in these wonderful woods and delightfully green countryside, in our ancestral lands where we are meant to be," O'Croake replied.

"May I ask you one last question, Mr Seamus O'Croake?" Hugo said, as the crow prepared to leave. "Where did Mr O'Dourves and Mr O'Driscoll go?"

"It is enough to say … *away*," O'Croake replied as he lifted off. "Now goodbye, and the two of you will ever be welcome in our home. Craw!!"

"You probably gathered, Cousin, that Mr Seamus O'Croake, head of the Boys in Black clan, will no longer be talking in yooman tongue and will be—" Hugo began to say.

"Staying here where they belong?" Sean added with a benign smile.

"Indeed," Hugo replied quietly. "His not talking to you, by the way, is not a slight on you. He is simply not communicating with humans directly, other than by the occasional cawing."

"I gathered that much," Sean said with a chuckle. "Perhaps one day, eh?"

-o-

"Can't we stay just a little bit longer?" Betsy begged as they settled into Grandpa Shylock's people carrier ready for the start of their journey home.

"But I thought you couldn't wait to be back home to your own little bed," Mamma Gwen said, not knowing how to take her daughter.

"That was then and this is … now," Betsy complained, the evidence of a tiny tear ready to sneak out of her eye corner. "I'm going to miss … everything."

Knowing her daughter extremely well, Gwen didn't doubt that as soon as something caught her eye *en route*, Betsy would forget about everything that had gone before. Her dad Josiah called her 'fickle', which couldn't have been closer to the truth.

"OK," Grandpa Shylock warned, "we need to set off. We've a lengthy drive ahead of us, and we have to find somewhere to consume those lovely sandwiches and home-baked coconut tarts your Granny Essie has prepared for lunch. All aboard for the *Skylark*!"

"Two hours and fifteen minutes," Hugo said. "And shouldn't that be *Stenaline*?"

"And what does all that mean when it's at home?" Betsy asked, not understanding what he was on about.

"It takes two hours and fifteen minutes to get to the ferry terminal, and the ship is called *Stenaline*, not *Skylark*," Hugo explained simply.

The adults in the group smiled indulgently, because that was typical of their young man – precise to the last full stop and crossed T.

"Time to be off then, Shylock?" Granny Essie said as she fastened her seat belt and sat back in the front seat next to her husband, ready for blast off.

"Write to me, Mandy, and I'll write back!" Betsy shouted through the open back window as they pulled away.

The morning was crisp and bright, with very few cottonwool clouds scudding across an azure sky. This was just the sort of a day that Hugo and his cousin Sean might have enjoyed, exploring the

CHAPTER TWELVE

woods further and stopping for an excellent corned beef sandwich or two, and tarts that Granny Essie would have prepared for them. It would have been topped by a giant flask of tea, too.

The week's events careered through Hugo's mind in the order they had happened, in the minutest of detail to their climax the day before. This young man took most things in his stride, unless something extraordinarily unusual or unexpected threw him off balance. Even then, the event would have to be almost impossible to floor him.

"OK, folks," Grandpa Shylock warned, as he pulled into a layby picnic spot. "Anyone fancy a bite to eat?"

"Yes, please, Grandpa!" Betsy shouted, her excitement overcoming her as she bounced up and down on her seat. "Thought you'd never ask. My belly was thinking my throat had been cut!"

The adults laughed out loud, recognising *that* saying as being one of Grandpa Shylock's.

"OK, then," he went on, once full mouths had halted conversations for a little while. "I have two little gifts for the youngsters among us."

"Yay!" Betsy shouted spraying crumbs from her mouthful of Victoria sponge. "Exciting!"

"Thank you, Grandpa," Hugo said in his usual quiet, grown-up sort of a way.

"However, you must promise that you will not open them until you are on the ferry, steaming your way back to Wales," Grandpa Shylock said quite firmly. "Promise?"

"Promise, Grandpa," Hugo agreed seriously. "Thank you for the gift. It's very kind of you. And thank you for the lovely food, Granny Essie."

"Aw, Gramps! Do I have to wait so long?" Betsy complained, shuffling her bottom on the bench at the picnic table, her feet underneath it. "Can't I have just a little peek?"

"You heard what Grandpa said, Betsy," Hugo butted in, rounding on his sister. "Can't you wait just a short time?"

"Aw!" she harrumphed, tapping her feet in mild annoyance. If there was one thing she didn't like, it was having to wait.

-o-

As soon as she had boarded the ferry, Betsy opened her present from Grandpa Shylock and Granny Essie. Much to her delight, she found a delicate gold chain with a golden acorn pendant, to remind her of her time spent among their wonderful oak trees.

Although she badgered her brother to open his, he refused, preferring not to share his joy with anyone else.

Half way into the three-and-a-half-hour journey, Hugo found himself alone at the stern of the ship. He half expected to catch a glimpse of Mr Seamus O'Croake and his boys trailing them to their destination, but to no avail.

It was then that he decided to see what his grandpa had wrapped up for him. He removed the outer wrapping very carefully to find a box beautifully covered with real oak leaves. Inside the box he discovered a single primary feather from a crow's wing, with a little note that said:

If ever you feel you need to be in Glenbower Wood to spend time with your friends, the Boys in Black, simply whisper over this feather the three magic words – Mr Seamus O'Croake – and there you will be, in the blink of his clever eye.

Frank English
Author

Born in 1946 in the West Riding of Yorkshire's coal fields around Wakefield, he attended grammar school, where he enjoyed sport rather more than academic work. After three years at teacher training college in Leeds, he became a teacher in 1967. He spent a lot of time during his teaching career entertaining children of all ages, a large part of which was through telling stories, and encouraging them to escape into a world of imagination and wonder. Some of his most disturbed youngsters he found to be very talented poets, for example. He has always had a wicked sense of humour, which has blossomed only during the time he *has spent with his wife, Denise. This sense of humour also allowed many youngsters to survive often difficult and brutalising home environments.*

In 2006, he retired after forty years working in schools with young people who had significantly disrupted lives because of behaviour disorders and poor social adjustment, generally brought about through circumstances beyond their control. At the same time as moving from leafy lane suburban middle-class school teaching in Leeds to residential schooling for emotional and behavioural disturbance in the early 1990s, changed family circumstance provided the spur to achieve ambitions. Supported by his wife, Denise, he achieved a Master's degree in his mid-forties and a PhD at the age of fifty-six, because he had always wanted to do so.

Other children's books he has written to date:

Magic Parcel: The Awakening	*Published June 2010*
Magic Parcel: The Gathering Storm	*Published March 2011*
Magic Parcel: A New Dawn	*Published August 2012*
18 Mulberry Road	*Published September 2011*
25 Primrose Walk	*Published January 2013*
Autumn Adventures	*Published September 2013*
Winter Tales	*Published September 2014*
Towards Spring	*Published September 2016*
Juniper's Tale	*Published August 2018*
Honey	*Published January 2019*
The Story of Lemuel Pecker	*Published April 2019*
Josephine's Journey	*Published June 2019*
Holly's Prize	*Published April 2020*
Sara's Astonishing Story	*Published May 2020*
Garnett's Grand Getaway	*Published June 2020*

www.ingramcontent.com/pod-product-compliance
Lightning Source LLC
Chambersburg PA
CBHW071542080526
44588CB00011B/1758